Based on the picture
Julia Donaldson • A

GRUFFALO CRUMBLE

and
other
recipes

24 recipes from the deep dark wood

MACMILLAN CHILDREN'S BOOKS

Contents

Scrambled Snake and Other Breakfasts

Deep Dark Wood Dips and Other Snacks

Turned-Out Toes and Other Meals

Gruffalo Crumble and Other Sweet Treats

How to Use This Book: Guidelines for Grown-Ups

This book is all about having fun with food. It's perfect for introducing young Gruffalo fans to cooking and is full of great ideas for everyday meals, special treats and party snacks to share with family and friends.

Every step-by-step recipe has been specially designed for adults and children to use together. The instructions are for adults to follow, but there are stages in each recipe that are an ideal opportunity to get a child involved – look out for the JOIN IN! Gruffalo paw.

The steps in the recipe that aren't marked with a JOIN IN! Gruffalo paw may be unsafe or complicated for a child, so it's recommended that you do those yourself. Keep a close eye on children in the kitchen at all times, and be especially careful of anything hot or sharp.

All oven temperatures are based on a fan oven, so you'll need to add about 20°C if you have a conventional oven.

You'll see a Tips, Tricks and Twists section on most pages, where you can find helpful hints and possible alternatives to try, so have fun and experiment!

Before you get started, read the hints and tips on the next page with your child.

Hints and Tips to Read Together

Is your tummy beginning to rumble? Are you ready to make lots of tasty treats from the deep dark wood? Here are a few hints and tips to help you get started.

- Remember to wash your hands so they're nice and clean. Cooking can get messy, so put on an apron and tie your hair back if it's long.

- Before you start, read the recipe together so you can make sure you have everything you need. You might find it helpful to weigh, measure or count out your ingredients so they are ready to use.

- Always wash fruit and vegetables before you cook or eat them.

- Be careful of anything hot – remember things that have just come out of the oven or off the hob will take a while to cool down, so don't touch. Ouch!

- Sharp knives are for grown-ups only.

- Lots of these recipes will ask you mix, squash or shape using your hands. Make sure you wash them before and afterwards, especially if you've used raw meat or egg.

- Not all uncooked ingredients or mixtures are safe to eat, so check with a grown-up first.

- You can get stuck in and help every time you see the JOIN IN! Gruffalo paw, so keep your eyes open, roll your sleeves up and get ready to have some fun!

JOIN IN!   It looks like this!

Breakfasts

Mouse Toast

Terrible Tusks

Purple Prickle Pancakes

Caterpillar Twists

Scrambled Snake

Mouse Toast

"My favourite food!" the Gruffalo said.
"You'll taste good on a slice of bread!"

Makes
1
mouse

You will need:

Butter
1 egg
1 black olive
2 chives
1 slice of ham
1 cherry tomato
1 slice of bread

A big circle cutter
   (7cm diameter)
A small circle cutter
   (3cm diameter)
A baking tray

What to do:

1 Preheat the oven to 180°C/Gas Mark 4.

JOIN IN! 2 Dip a piece of kitchen roll in butter and rub it all over the baking tray.

JOIN IN! 3 Press the big circle cutter into the bread and make sure you cut all the way through.

JOIN IN! 4 Lift out the circle of bread. You don't need it and can eat it as a snack.

JOIN IN! 5 The hole in the bread is Mouse's face. Now use the small circle cutter to make ears.

JOIN IN! 6 Put the slice of bread on the baking tray and press down very firmly.

7 Butter the bread.

JOIN IN! 8 Break the egg into a saucer and pick out any pieces of shell.

9 Carefully slide the egg into the hole and bake in the oven for 6 minutes.

10 While you're waiting, get your decorations ready: cut an olive in half to be Mouse's eyes, and cut a cherry tomato in half for a nose.

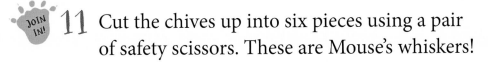 11 Cut the chives up into six pieces using a pair of safety scissors. These are Mouse's whiskers!

12 Cut two small circles out of a slice of ham to make round pink ears.

13 Take the toast out of the oven and transfer to a plate.

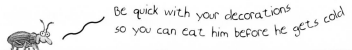 14 Decorate Mouse! You can copy the picture below.

Be quick with your decorations so you can eat him before he gets cold

Tips, Tricks and Twists

- Make sure you press the bread down really firmly on the buttered baking tray so that the egg stays in the hole.

- You can bake your egg for an extra minute if you don't want a runny yolk.

- If you don't want to use ham for the ears, try halved cherry tomatoes instead.

Terrible Tusks

Make your very own Gruffalo tusks using
lots of different kinds of fruit.

Makes 8 tusks

You will need:

4 bananas
3 or 4 different
  kinds of soft fruit:
  try strawberries,
  melon and kiwi

Drinking straws

What to do:

1 Cut the soft fruit into bite-size pieces and lay everything out on a big plate or tray.

2 Chop each banana into three equal pieces. Keep the curved ends to one side.

3 Chop up the remaining middle sections and add to the plate of fruit.

JOIN IN! 4 Take a drinking straw.

JOIN IN! 5 One by one, slide pieces of fruit onto the straw. Mix up different sizes, shapes and colours.

JOIN IN! 6 Finish off your tusk with the curved end of a banana.

Tips, Tricks and Twists

- Make sure the fruit is really soft and ripe, or it will be difficult to slide onto the straws.

- You can use any fruit you like! It's nice to use a mixture of different colours. Here are some ideas:

RED
Strawberries
Watermelon

GREEN
Green grapes
Kiwi
Melon

ORANGE
Mango
Orange
Apricot

YELLOW
Pineapple
Peach

I bet your fingers are really sticky!

Purple Prickle Pancakes

He has purple prickles all over his back
– just like these delicious pancakes.

Makes 10 Pancakes

You will need:

1 egg
200ml milk
220g plain flour
$^1/_2$ teaspoon
   bicarbonate of soda
2 teaspoons honey
$^1/_4$ teaspoon
   cinnamon
50 blueberries
A knob of butter

A big mixing bowl
A measuring jug
A frying pan
A spatula
A small ladle
A whisk

What to do:

 1 Put the flour, bicarbonate of soda and cinnamon in the big bowl and mix well. These are your dry ingredients.

 2 Pour the milk into a measuring jug and add the honey. Stir together.

 3 Break the egg into a saucer and pick out any pieces of shell.

 4 Add the egg to the measuring jug and mix well with a fork.

 5 Make a little well in the middle of the dry ingredients and pour in the milk mixture.

 6 Mix everything well with a whisk until you have a thick batter with no lumps.

7 Melt a little butter in the frying pan on a high heat.

8   When the pan is really hot, add the batter one ladle at a time and drop five blueberries in each heap of batter.

9   Flip the pancakes over when little bubbles appear on top.

10   Cook until they are brown on the second side, then put them on a plate and cover with foil to keep warm.
Keep going until you've used up all the mixture.

Can you count out five blueberries for each pancake?

Tips, Tricks and Twists

● These are really delicious served with a little honey or maple syrup drizzled on top.

● The Gruffalo's Child has pink prickles on her back. If you use raspberries instead of blueberries, these pancakes will have pink prickles too!

Caterpillar Twists

There are lots of caterpillars in the deep dark wood.
These make a very chocolatey breakfast treat.

Makes 10 caterpillars

You will need:

1 sheet ready-made
   puff pastry (350g)
3 tablespoons
   chocolate spread
20 white chocolate
   buttons
Extra butter for
   greasing

A baking tray
A butter knife
A sharp knife

What to do:

1 Preheat the oven to 200°C/Gas Mark 6.

JOIN IN!
2 Dip a piece of kitchen roll in butter and
   rub it all over the baking tray.

3 Lay out the sheet of puff pastry with one
   of the short ends towards you. Cut it in
   half widthways with a sharp knife, so you
   have two smaller sheets.

JOIN IN!
4 Smear chocolate spread all over one sheet
   using a butter knife. Make sure you go
   right to the edges!

5 Carefully put the other sheet on top of
   the chocolate-covered one.

6 Cut into ten strips.

JOIN IN!
7 Pick up one of the strips. Hold each end
   and twist it until you have a spiral, then
   place carefully on the baking tray. Repeat
   with the other strips.

8 Bake for 15-20 minutes until golden brown.

JOIN IN!

9 Allow to cool for 10 minutes, then place two chocolate buttons on the end of each caterpillar twist as eyes. The caterpillars should still be warm enough for the chocolate to melt and stick to the pastry.

10 Finish off each eye with a blob of chocolate spread.

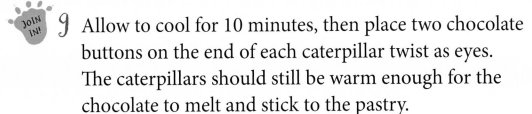

These could make a great party snack too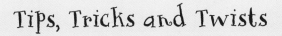

Tips, Tricks and Twists

● If you can't get the chocolate buttons to stay on the pastry, try sticking them down with a small blob of chocolate spread.

● You could give these a citrus twist by sprinkling some grated orange zest over the chocolate.

Hello friends!

Scrambled Snake

*"Scrambled snake! It's time I hid.
Goodbye little mouse," and away Snake slid.*

Makes
2
servings

You will need:

5 eggs
1 tablespoon milk
A knob of butter
2 tablespoons
    fresh herbs
2 slices of bread
A pinch of salt

A medium-sized bowl
A heavy-bottomed
    saucepan

What to do:

JOIN IN! 1 Cut up the herbs as finely as you can using a pair of safety scissors. Watch your fingers!

JOIN IN! 2 Break the eggs into the bowl and pick out any pieces of shell.

JOIN IN! 3 Add the milk and salt.

JOIN IN! 4 Mix with a fork until all the yolks have broken and you have a smooth pale yellow mixture.

5 Melt the butter in a pan over a low heat. Tip in the egg mixture and cook until set, stirring continuously.

6 Stir in the herbs and watch your eggs turn green!

7 Toast the bread, and butter it if you wish.

8 Transfer everything to a plate.

JOIN IN! 9 Garnish with a few more chopped herbs.

Eat it quickly before it gets cold!

Tips, Tricks and Twists

● There are lots of green herbs you could use. You could try parsley, chives, coriander or dill.

● Instead of herbs, why not add something else to turn your mixture green, like pesto, spinach or cress.

● If you're really hungry, you could add something extra. Try mushrooms, ham or grated cheese.

● For every extra person, add two more eggs, a splash more milk and another tablespoon of herbs.

Snacks

Frog Muffins

Snake's Logpile House

Woodland Salad

Orange Eyes

Deep Dark Wood Dips with
Terrible Teeth Tortillas

Swirly Snails

Fox's Sandwiches

Frog Muffins

These savoury muffins are really green, and you can decorate them to look just like frogs.

Makes
8
muffins

You will need:

100g raw spinach
150g plain flour
1 teaspoon baking
  powder
75g grated cheese
30g butter
100ml milk
A pinch of salt
2 eggs
8 teaspoons
  cream cheese
8 black olives, halved
A slice of ham

A muffin tray
8 paper cases
A food processor
A large mixing bowl
A measuring jug

What to do:

1 Preheat the oven to 180°C/Gas Mark 4.

2 Put eight paper cases in a muffin tray.

3 Blend the spinach in the food processor until smooth.

4 Sift the flour and baking powder into the large mixing bowl. Add the cheese and salt and stir together.

5 Melt the butter over a low heat and leave to cool.

6 Break the eggs into a small bowl and pick out any pieces of shell.

7 Put the milk, spinach, eggs and butter in the measuring jug. Mix well with a fork.

JOIN IN! **8** Make a little well in the middle of the dry mixture in the bowl and pour in the contents of the jug. Mix everything really well.

9 Divide the mixture evenly between the paper cases and cook for 15-18 minutes.

JOIN IN! **10** While the muffins are baking, cut the ham into thin strips using a pair of safety scissors. These will be the frogs' tongues!

11 When the muffins are baked, leave them to cool down. Cut a groove in each one to be a mouth.

JOIN IN! **12** Put two blobs of cream cheese above the mouth and add a halved olive to each one to make froggy eyes. Then put a ham tongue in the mouth. You can copy the picture below.

Tips, Tricks and Twists

● You could use a thin strip of red pepper as a tongue instead of ham.

Snake's Logpile House

You can make two kinds of celery snack and stack them up to make your very own logpile house.

Makes 12 logs

You will need:

4 sticks of celery
6 tablespoons
  peanut butter
2 tablespoons raisins
6 tablespoons
  cream cheese
1 tablespoon
  poppy seeds

A butter knife

What to do:

1 Cut each celery stick into three so you have twelve equal-sized pieces.

JOIN IN! 2 Take six of the pieces and lay them down so the hollow side is facing up.

3 Put a tablespoon of peanut butter on each piece.

JOIN IN! 4 Use the butter knife to smear the peanut butter across the celery until it fills up the hollow part.

JOIN IN! 5 Put a few raisins on each celery log. Press them gently into the peanut butter with your finger so they don't fall off.

JOIN IN! 6 Now take the other six pieces of celery and lay them down hollow-side up.

It looks like there are ants on the logs!

7   Put a tablespoon of cream cheese on each piece.

 8   Smear the cream cheese over the celery to fill the hollow, just like you did with the peanut butter.

 9   Sprinkle the poppy seeds all over the cheese.

 10   Here's the tricky bit! Try stacking up your logs to make a house – or you could just eat them as they are.

Tips, Tricks and Twists

- Can you think of anything else that you could fill the celery with? You could try hummus or one of the Deep Dark Wood Dips from page 28.

- If your logs are slipping and sliding when you're trying to stack them up, you can put a small blob of peanut butter or cream cheese on the bottom to stick them in place.

Woodland Salad

A mouse took a stroll through the deep dark wood . . .
Make your own edible forest!

Makes 2 salads

You will need:

8 shelled walnut halves
Salad leaves
1 carrot
1 cucumber
4 cherry tomatoes
40g cheddar cheese
2 teaspoons cream
   cheese

A sharp knife
A chopping board
A tree-shaped cutter
A cocktail stick

What to do:

 1 Break up the walnuts roughly into quarters. You can do this with your hands.

2 Cut the carrot into thin rounds. Use a sharp knife to cut away small triangles around the edge to make flower shapes.

3 Cut two 6cm lengths of cucumber. Now stand the lengths up on their ends and cut them into long rectangular slices.

 4 Lay out all the slices of cucumber on the chopping board.

 5 Use your cutters to make the cucumber slices into trees.

6 Put three big handfuls of salad leaves on each plate and arrange your flowers, trees and walnuts on top.

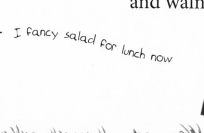

I fancy salad for lunch now

7   Cut the cheese into eight cubes about 1cm square and cut the cherry tomatoes in half.

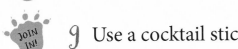

8   Put four cubes of cheese on each plate.

9   Use a cocktail stick to dot small blobs of cream cheese on the tops of the halved tomatoes. This is quite tricky and you might need some help!

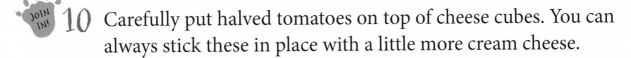

10   Carefully put halved tomatoes on top of cheese cubes. You can always stick these in place with a little more cream cheese.

Tips, Tricks and Twists

Yum!

- Make sure you wash all your salad vegetables before you start.

- If you don't have tree cutters, you can ask a grown-up to cut the shapes with a sharp knife.

- You could use radishes instead of carrots to make pink flowers.

- Why not drizzle a little olive oil or dressing on top?

Orange Eyes

His eyes are orange . . .
and so are these little cheese tarts.

Makes
12
tarts

You will need:

150g flour
75g soft butter
3 tablespoons water
100g grated cheese
2 eggs
5 tablespoons milk
6 black olives, halved
Extra butter for
  greasing

A muffin tray
A large mixing bowl
A rolling pin
A circle cutter
  (7cm diameter)
A measuring jug

What to do:

1 Preheat the oven to 180°C/Gas Mark 4.

JOIN IN!
2 Dip a piece of kitchen paper in some butter and grease the holes in the muffin tray.

JOIN IN!
3 Put the flour in the large mixing bowl. Add the butter bit by bit and rub together with your fingers to make crumbs.

JOIN IN!
4 Add the water and squash everything into a ball. If it's a bit too sticky, you can add a little more flour. This is your pastry.

5 Sprinkle a little flour on a clean surface and roll out the pastry until it's about ½ cm thick.

JOIN IN!
6 Press the round cutter into the pastry to make twelve circles.

JOIN IN!
7 Put each circle of pastry in a hole in the muffin tray and press it down firmly.

Why not pick a cheese that's orange in colour

JOIN IN! 8 Break the eggs into the measuring jug and pick out any bits of shell.

JOIN IN! 9 Add the milk and grated cheese and mix well with a fork.

10 Pour the mixture into the pastry cases.

JOIN IN! 11 Drop one halved olive into the middle of each tart.

12 Cook for 12-15 minutes. You can eat these hot or cold.

Tips, Tricks and Twists

● You can make your tarts more filling by replacing half of the cheese with another ingredient, such as sweetcorn, tuna or ham.

● If you don't like olives, how about using raisins instead?

Wow, they look so real!

Deep Dark Wood Dips
with Terrible Teeth Tortillas

Guacamole

You will need:

2 very ripe avocados
1 teaspoon lemon juice
A pinch of salt
A handful of fresh coriander

A shallow bowl
A potato masher

What to do:

JOIN IN!

1 Cut up the coriander with a pair of safety scissors, as finely as you can.

2 Halve the avocados and remove the stones.

JOIN IN!

3 Using a spoon, scoop out the flesh into the shallow bowl.

JOIN IN!

4 Mash with a potato masher until smooth.

JOIN IN!

5 Add the lemon juice, coriander and salt and give everything a good stir.

6 Put your guacamole in a clean bowl to serve.

These dips are also delicious with crunchy raw vegetables like cucumber, carrot or red pepper

Minty Yoghurt

You will need:

250ml Greek yoghurt
A handful of fresh mint
A quarter of a cucumber
1 teaspoon lemon juice

What to do:

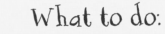 1 Cut up the mint with a pair of safety scissors, as finely as you can.

2 Finely chop the cucumber.

3 Put the yoghurt in a bowl with the cucumber and lemon juice.

4 Add the mint and stir.

Terrible Teeth Tortillas

You will need:

2 plain wraps
Olive oil

A pastry brush
A baking tray

What to do:

1 Preheat the oven to 180°C/Gas Mark 4.

2 Cut the wraps into triangles and squares with a pair of safety scissors and lay on a baking tray.

3 Brush with a little oil and bake for 5 minutes.

Swirly Snails

Make your own delicious snails using this simple dough recipe.

Makes
12
snails

You will need:

250g plain flour
1 teaspoon baking
   powder
65g butter
120ml milk
2 tablespoons pesto
4 tablespoons grated
   cheese
Extra butter for
   greasing

A baking tray
A large mixing bowl
A rolling pin
Cocktail sticks

What to do:

1 Preheat the oven to 180°C/Gas Mark 4.

2 Dip a piece of kitchen paper in some butter and grease the baking tray.

3 Sift the flour and baking powder into the large mixing bowl and stir.

4 Add the butter bit by bit and rub between your fingers until combined.

5 Pour in the milk and mix with your hands to make a soft, squashy dough.

6 Sprinkle a little flour on a clean surface and roll out the pastry. Aim for a rectangular shape that's 25cm long and 12cm wide.

7 Trim the edges to make a neat rectangle. Save the leftover pieces for later.

8 Evenly spread the pesto all over the rectangle of dough, but leave about 2cm clean along one long edge.

 9 Sprinkle the cheese all over the pesto, making sure to avoid the clean strip of dough.

10 Roll up the rectangle into a tight sausage. Start at the long edge that is covered in pesto and cheese. Leave the clean strip of dough poking out at the end – it will be the snails' heads.

11 Cut the dough sausage into twelve thick slices to make snails.

12 Use the leftover pieces of dough from earlier to make eyes. Roll into balls and stick on the snails' heads with a little milk.

13 Stand the snails on the baking tray. You can put a cocktail stick down the middle of each snail to hold it together.

14 Cook for 25 minutes until golden brown.

Tips, Tricks and Twists

- Take the butter out of the fridge at least half an hour before you start. That way it will be nice and soft, so it will be easier to make your dough.

- You could use tomato purée instead of pesto to make cheese and tomato snails.

Fox's Sandwiches

"It's Fox," said the mouse. "Why, Fox, hello!"

Makes
1
sandwich

You will need:

1 slice of bread
Cream cheese
1 slice of
    orange cheese
2 slices of cucumber
2 black olives, halved
2 chives

A circle cutter
    (8cm diameter)
A sharp knife
A butter knife

What to do:

JOIN IN! **1** Press your circle cutter into the bread and take out the round piece. You don't need the rest.

JOIN IN! **2** Spread the round piece of bread with cream cheese using a butter knife.

JOIN IN! **3** Press your circle cutter into the slice of orange cheese and take out the round piece. You don't need the rest.

JOIN IN! **4** Now cut the round piece of cheese into the shape of fox's face. Cut away a leaf-shaped section from either side with your cutter.

JOIN IN! **5** You will now have three pieces of cheese: one big, and two small. Carefully place the big piece of cheese on top of the cream cheese.

6   Cut one of the small pieces of cheese in half. You don't need the other piece.

JOIN IN!

7   Place the cheese halves at the top of the fox's face to make his ears.

8   Use a sharp knife to cut two slices of cucumber.

JOIN IN!

9   Use a pair of safety scissors to cut the chives into six pieces.

JOIN IN!

10   Now decorate your fox! Two slices of cucumber and two halved olives for the eyes, chives for whiskers and another halved olive for a shiny black nose.

Tips, Tricks and Twists

- Look carefully at the picture of the finished sandwich before you start. You can copy it as you follow the instructions.

- You can eat the spare pieces of bread and cheese as a snack.

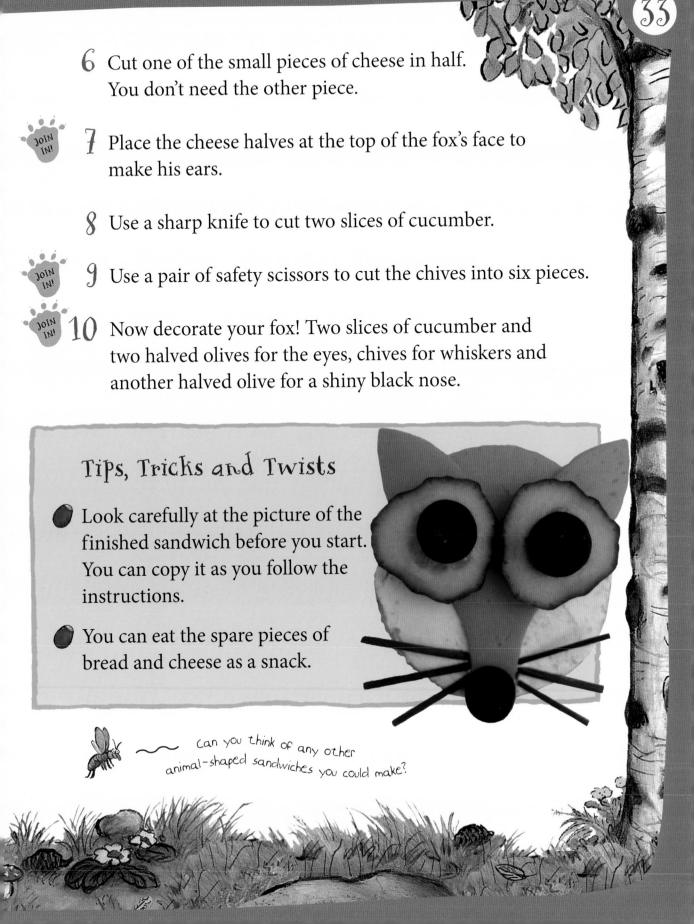

Can you think of any other animal-shaped sandwiches you could make?

Meals

Toadstool Pizza

Turned-Out Toes

Poisonous Warts

Potato Owls

Roasted Fox

Toadstool Pizza

These cheese and tomato pizzas
look just like toadstools.

Makes
6
Pizzas

You will need:

200g flour
2 teaspoons baking
    powder
A pinch of salt
1 teaspoon dried
    herbs
1 tablespoon olive oil
120ml warm water
6 tablespoons tomato
    sauce
6 mini mozzarella
    balls
Extra olive oil for
    greasing

A baking tray
A large mixing bowl
A rolling pin
A circle cutter
    (8-10cm diameter)

What to do:

1 Preheat the oven to 220°C/Gas Mark 7.

 2 Dip a piece of kitchen paper in a little olive oil and grease the baking tray.

 3 Put the flour, baking powder, salt and herbs in the large mixing bowl and stir.

 4 Make a little well in the middle and add the tablespoon of olive oil.

 5 Pour in the water a little at a time and mix with a spoon until you have a soft dough.

 6 Use your hands to squash the dough into a ball and knead it for a minute or two.

7 Sprinkle a little flour on a clean surface and roll out the dough until it's about ½ cm thick.

 8 Use the circle cutter to press six circles out of the dough.

9 Use a knife to cut away two sections of each circle so you have a toadstool shape. You can copy the picture below.

10 Cut the mozzarella balls into slices about ½ cm thick.

JOIN IN! 11 Lay the toadstool pizza bases on the baking tray, not too close together.

JOIN IN! 12 Put a tablespoon of tomato sauce on each pizza and spread it around with the back of the spoon. Leave the toadstool stump clean!

JOIN IN! 13 Dot the mozzarella slices over each toadstool.

14 Cook for 12-15 minutes.

Tips, Tricks and Twists

● You can wrap the leftover dough in cling film and keep it in the fridge for a few days.

● How about adding something extra to your toadstool pizzas? Try mushrooms, sweetcorn, ham . . . or anything else you can think of!

You shouldn't eat real toadstools – they're sometimes poisonous!

Turned-Out Toes

These mini burgers make excellent Gruffalo paws, complete with turned-out toes.

Makes 6 burgers

You will need:

200g lean beef mince
A handful of parsley
1 egg
2 tablespoons
   breadcrumbs
30 pine nuts

A large mixing bowl
A muffin tray

What to do:

1 Preheat the oven to 220°C/Gas Mark 7.

2 Put the mince in the large mixing bowl.

JOIN IN! 3 Cut up the parsley with a pair of safety scissors and add to the mince.

JOIN IN! 4 Break the egg into a small saucer and pick out any pieces of shell.

JOIN IN! 5 Tip the egg into the mixing bowl and add the breadcrumbs.

JOIN IN! 6 Mix everything really thoroughly with your hands. Wash them carefully first!

JOIN IN! 7 Put six handfuls of the mixture into the muffin tray, one handful in each hole.

I'm going to nibble the toes first

8 Squash down the mixture with your hands. Make sure you wash them afterwards.

 9 Stick five pine nuts firmly into each burger as toes.

10 Bake for 15-20 minutes.

These are best served hot

Tips, Tricks and Twists

- Make sure you wash your hands before and after handling raw meat, and don't eat any of the uncooked mixture.

- It's best to use lean mince for this recipe. If the mince is too fatty, the fat will rise to the surface when cooking.

- Why not serve these burgers with Roasted Fox? See page 44 for the recipe.

Poisonous Warts

Don't worry, these frittatas won't poison you –
they're made with peas, not warts!

Makes 8 frittatas

You will need:

4 eggs
60g feta cheese
3 chives
10 teaspoons peas
Extra butter for
  greasing

A muffin tray
A measuring jug

What to do:

1 Preheat the oven to 180°C/Gas Mark 4.

JOIN IN! 2 Dip a piece of kitchen paper in some butter and grease the holes in the muffin tray.

JOIN IN! 3 Break the eggs into the measuring jug and pick out any pieces of shell.

JOIN IN! 4 Cut up the chives into little pieces using a pair of safety scissors. Add to the egg mixture.

JOIN IN! 5 Use your fingers to crumble up the feta cheese and add it to the mixture.

JOIN IN! 6 Mix everything really well with a fork.

7 Pour the mixture into eight holes in the muffin tray.

Easy peasy!

8 Add a teaspoon of peas to each one.

9 Cook for 12-15 minutes.

10 Run a butter knife around the edge of each frittata and then carefully lift them out.

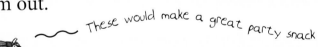

These would make a great party snack

Tips, Tricks and Twists

- Make sure you grease the muffin tray really thoroughly so the frittatas don't stick.

- You don't have to use feta cheese – why not try grated cheddar or parmesan instead?

Potato Owls

Decorate these cheesy baked
potatoes to look like Owl.

Makes
4
owls

You will need:

2 large baking
 potatoes
1 tin tuna (150g),
 drained
1 tablespoon milk
A knob of butter
Olive oil
100g grated cheese
4 black olives, sliced
2 slices yellow cheese
1 slice orange cheese
8 small lettuce leaves

A baking tray
A shallow bowl
A potato masher
A circle cutter
 (2-3cm diameter)

What to do:

1 Preheat the oven to 220°C/Gas Mark 7.

JOIN IN!
2 Dip a piece of kitchen roll in a little olive
 oil and rub all over the baking tray.

3 Cut the potatoes in half lengthways so
 you have four ovals. Put them on the
 baking tray flat side up and brush with
 a little oil.

4 Bake for 40-50 minutes until soft in the
 middle. Take out of the oven and leave
 to cool. Don't switch the oven off.

5 Use a spoon to scoop out the middle of
 the potato and put in the shallow bowl.
 Keep the skins to one side for later.

JOIN IN!
6 Add the milk and butter to the potatoes
 and mash with a potato masher
 until soft and fluffy.

7 Add the tuna and half the cheese to the mashed potato and mix well.

 8 Spoon the mixture back into the potato skins and sprinkle the leftover cheese on top.

9 Put the filled skins back in the oven for 5-10 minutes until golden and melty.

 10 While they're cooking, press the small circle cutter into the yellow cheese slices eight times. These will be the eyes.

11 Cut a slice of orange cheese into four triangles to make beaks.

12 Take the potato owls out of the oven and put them on plates.

 13 Decorate them quickly with eyes and beaks. Use lettuce leaves as wings.

Tips, Tricks and Twists

- As the tin of tuna has sharp edges, it's a good idea to empty the drained tuna into a small bowl before giving to a child to add to the potato mixture.

- You can use any cheese you like, or even a mixture of cheeses.

- You could try raisins for the eyes or carrot as a beak.

Roasted Fox

"Roasted fox! I'm off!" Fox said.
"Goodbye, little mouse," and away he sped.

Makes
4
servings

You will need:

2 medium sweet
 potatoes (400g)
½ teaspoon cumin
½ teaspoon cinnamon
½ teaspoon salt
½ teaspoon black
 pepper
1 tablespoon oil
Extra oil for greasing

A baking tray
A small bowl
A large mixing bowl

What to do:

1 Preheat the oven to 180°C/Gas Mark 4.

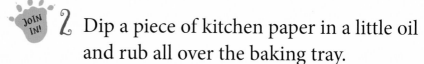

2 Dip a piece of kitchen paper in a little oil and rub all over the baking tray.

3 Peel the sweet potatoes and chop them into wedges around 10cm long and 1-2cm wide. Put in the large mixing bowl.

4 Put the cumin, cinnamon, salt and black pepper in the small bowl and mix well with a spoon.

5 Add the tablespoon of oil to the spices and mix again.

6 Tip the mixture over the wedges. Make sure you scrape every last bit out of the bowl.

 7 Give everything a really good mix so the wedges are coated in the mixture. It's best to use your hands!

 8 Put the coated wedges on the baking tray.

9 Bake for 15 minutes, and then give the tray a little shake. Put back in the oven for another 10-15 minutes.

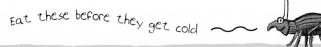

Eat these before they get cold

Tips, Tricks and Twists

- If you don't want to use sweet potato, why not try butternut squash, halved carrots or even a mixture.

- You can leave out the spices if you prefer and just use salt and pepper.

- Why not eat these with Turned-Out Toes (page 38)?

- You could try these with a dollop of Minty Yoghurt (page 29).

crikey, he's in a hurry!

Sweet Treats

Gruffalo Crumble

Mouse's Nut and Date Bars

Berry Jellies

Knobbly Knees

Owl Ice Cream

Gingerbread Mice

Gruffalo Cake

Gruffalo Crumble

"Gruffalo crumble!" the Gruffalo said,
And quick as the wind he turned and fled.

Makes
6
helpings

You will need:

3 eating apples
1 teaspoon
   cinnamon
1 tablespoon
   caster sugar
1 tablespoon
   apple juice
300g blackberries
75g unsalted butter
100g plain flour
50g oats
50g brown sugar

Two large mixing
   bowls
A baking dish
   (about 15 x 20cm)

What to do:

1 Preheat the oven to 180°C/Gas Mark 4.

2 Peel and core the apples, then chop them into bite-size pieces.

JOIN IN! 3 Put the chopped apples and blackberries in a large mixing bowl. Save a handful of blackberries for later.

JOIN IN! 4 Add the cinnamon, caster sugar and apple juice and give everything a good stir.

5 Tip the fruit mixture into the baking dish.

6 Cut the butter into small cubes of around 1cm.

JOIN IN! 7 Put the butter in the other large mixing bowl and add the flour.

JOIN IN! 8 Use your fingers to rub the butter and flour together until the mixture looks like crumbs.

9 Stir in the oats and brown sugar.

 10 Sprinkle the mixture over the fruit in the baking dish. Try and cover it as evenly as you can.

 11 Stick the remaining blackberries into the top of the crumble to decorate.

12 Cook for 40 minutes.

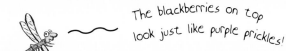

The blackberries on top look just like purple prickles!

Tips, Tricks and Twists

- It's best to use cold butter for this recipe – warm butter can easily become a dough rather than the crumbs you need.

- Why not try different fruits for the filling, like pear, peach or blueberries – or even a mixture.

- Gruffalo Crumble is best served hot. For an extra treat, you could eat it with ice cream or custard.

Mouse's Nut and Date Bars

All was quiet in the deep dark wood.
The mouse found a nut, and the nut was good.

Makes
12
bars

You will need:

225g dates
150g unsalted butter
5 tablespoons honey
150g oats
150g chopped nuts
150g raisins
4 tablespoons mixed
  seeds
Extra butter for
  greasing

A food processor
A small saucepan
A large mixing bowl
An oven tray
  (about 20 x 30cm)

What to do:

1 Preheat the oven to 180°C/Gas Mark 4.

 JOIN IN!

2 Dip a piece of kitchen paper in butter and rub all over the oven tray.

3 Finely chop the dates in the food processor until they become sticky crumbs.

4 Melt the butter and honey in a pan. Pour into the large mixing bowl and leave to cool.

5 Add the dates and mix really well.

JOIN IN!

6 Mix in the oats, nuts, seeds and raisins. You might need to use your hands! The mixture should be quite stiff.

JOIN IN!

7 Tip the mixture into the oven tray and spread it out evenly.

I can't wait to try one of these!

JOIN IN!

8 Squash down the mixture with your hands. You will need to be quite firm. It should be really compact when you've finished.

9 Bake for 20-25 minutes until golden brown on top.

10 Allow to cool. When completely cold, chop into squares to serve.

Tips, Tricks and Twists

- You can use any nuts you like, such as pistachios, hazelnuts, pecans, walnuts, peanuts or cashews – or a mixture.

- If you don't want to use nuts, try swapping with an extra 150g of oats.

- Why not try chopped apricots instead of raisins?

Yum!

Berry Jellies

Use your favourite berries to make these delicious jellies.

Makes
6
Jellies

You will need:

6 sheets gelatine
400ml apple juice
100ml water
18 raspberries
12 blueberries

A shallow bowl
A small saucepan
A muffin tray with
   six holes

What to do:

JOIN IN! 1 Lay the gelatine sheets in the shallow bowl and cover with warm water from the tap. Leave for a few minutes until soft.

JOIN IN! 2 Lift the gelatine sheets out of the bowl and squeeze them with your hands. This will get rid of some of the water.

3 Put the gelatine sheets in the small saucepan and add the apple juice and 100ml of water.

4 Heat gently until the gelatine sheets have dissolved.

JOIN IN! 5 Put three raspberries in each hole in the muffin tray.

JOIN IN! 6 Add two blueberries to each hole.

7 Pour the warm mixture into the six holes of the muffin tray.

8 Put in the fridge to set.
It will take around 2-3 hours.

9 When set, run around the edges of the jellies
with a butter knife and turn out onto a plate.

Tips, Tricks and Twists

- You might prefer to buy powdered gelatine in a sachet – just follow the instructions on the packet for 500ml of liquid.

- It's easier to turn out the set jellies if you sit the muffin tray in a few centimetres of warm water for 5 minutes first.

- Why not try different fruit, like blackberries, cherries or halved strawberries?

This is so wobbly!

Knobbly Knees

He has knobbly knees . . .
These crunchy cakes are nice and knobbly too!

Makes **12** cakes

You will need:

25g unsalted butter
100g chocolate
75g cornflakes
25g nuts
25g raisins
2 tablespoons honey

A small saucepan
A big bowl
12 paper cases
A muffin tray

What to do:

1 Break the chocolate into pieces with your hands and put in the small saucepan.

2 Add the butter and honey.

3 Melt over a low heat. Stir until everything is combined and leave to cool.

4 Put the cornflakes, nuts and raisins in the big bowl. These are your dry ingredients.

5 Mix the dry ingredients together.

6 Pour the warm contents of the pan over the dry ingredients.

7 Mix everything together really well. It should be quite stiff.

8 Put 12 paper cases in the muffin tray.

JOIN IN!

9 Divide the mixture evenly between the paper cases. You can use a tablespoon to scoop it out of the bowl, and then scrape the mixture into the paper case using a teaspoon.

10 Put in the fridge for 2 hours to set.

Tips, Tricks and Twists

- You can use any kind of nuts you like, or for a treat you could swap them with mini marshmallows.

- If you want to get messy, you can mix everything together with your hands – otherwise use a wooden spoon!

Owl Ice Cream

"Owl ice cream? Toowhit toowhoo!
Goodbye, little mouse," and away Owl flew.

Makes
6
ice creams

You will need:

4 bananas
1 teaspoon cinnamon
3 tablespoons flaked
   almonds
2 tablespoons raisins

A baking tray
A food processor
A medium-sized
   mixing bowl
6 small yoghurt pots
6 lolly sticks
A baking dish

What to do:

1 Break up the bananas into pieces about 2cm long. You can do this with your hands.

2 Put the banana pieces on a baking tray in the freezer for 2-3 hours.

3 Take the banana pieces out of the freezer and put them in the food processor.

4 Blend until thick, smooth and creamy. This may take a few minutes. Tip into the mixing bowl.

5 Stir in the cinnamon, raisins and flaked almonds.

6 Evenly divide the mixture between the six yoghurt pots.

7 Slide a lolly stick into each yoghurt pot, as straight as you can. Try and get it in the middle.

8 Put the pots back in the freezer for an hour.

Brr!

9 Fill the baking dish with warm water.
After taking the pots out of the freezer, dip them
in the water for a few seconds to loosen the ice cream.

JOIN IN! 10 Take hold of the lolly stick and gently pull out your ice
cream. Eat it quickly before it melts!

Tips, Tricks and Twists

You can add anything you like to your frozen banana mixture,
so get creative and make up your own delicious flavours.
Here are some ideas:

Mango   Chopped nuts   Raspberries
Chocolate chips   Peanut butter   Vanilla
Dried coconut   Honey

Gingerbread Mice

Make some friends for Mouse
with this easy gingerbread recipe.

Makes 12 mice

You will need:

60g unsalted butter
50g brown sugar
2 tablespoons honey
150g plain flour
½ teaspoon
    bicarbonate of soda
1 teaspoon ground
    ginger
12 raisins
6 dried cranberries
12 peanuts
Extra butter for
    greasing

A baking tray
A small saucepan
A large mixing bowl
A butter knife

What to do:

1 Preheat the oven to 180°C/Gas Mark 4.

JOIN IN! 2 Dip a piece of kitchen paper in some butter and grease the baking tray.

3 Melt the butter, sugar and honey in the saucepan over a low heat. Leave to cool.

JOIN IN! 4 Mix the flour, bicarbonate of soda and ground ginger in the large mixing bowl.

5 Pour the warm butter mixture into the bowl. Make sure it's not too hot!

JOIN IN! 6 Mix with your hands to make a stiff dough. If it's too sticky, you can add a little more flour. If it feels too dry, add a splash of water.

JOIN IN! 7 Divide your dough into thirteen pieces and roll into balls. Put twelve on the baking tray and keep the thirteenth to one side.

8 Flatten the twelve balls with the palm of your hand and pinch into a teardrop shape. These are your mice.

 9 Roll out the last ball into a long, thin sausage and cut into twelve with a butter knife.

 10 Curl each little sausage into a snail shape to make the mice's tails. Stick one behind each mouse.

11 Cut the cranberries and raisins in half with a pair of scissors.

 12 Stick the halved raisins on as eyes, and a halved cranberry for a nose.

 13 Separate the peanuts in half. They should come apart easily. Press two halves into each mouse to make ears.

14 Bake for 5-8 minutes.

Tips, Tricks and Twists

- Make sure you leave lots of space between the mice on the baking tray as they will expand as they cook. You might even prefer to use two baking trays to be on the safe side.

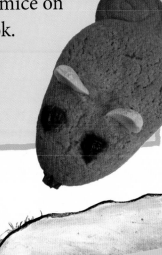

Gruffalo Cake

You will need:

200g unsalted butter (soft)
200g caster sugar
5 eggs
200g plain flour
4 tablespoons cocoa powder
3 teaspoons baking powder
Extra butter for greasing

A square cake tin (20cm x 20cm)
A large mixing bowl
A rubber spatula
A wire rack
A food processor

What to do:

Makes 16 servings

First make the cake:

1 Preheat the oven to 180°C/Gas Mark 4.

 2 Dip a piece of kitchen paper in some butter and grease the cake tin.

3 Cream the butter and sugar together in the food processor until pale and fluffy. Transfer to the large mixing bowl.

 4 Break the eggs into a small bowl and pick out any pieces of shell.

 5 Add the eggs to the butter and sugar and mix well.

 6 Sieve the flour, baking powder and cocoa into the mixture. Fold in with a spatula.

7 Pour the mixture into the tin and bake for 40-45 minutes. Check if it's cooked by inserting a knife. It should come out clean.

8 Remove the cake from the tin and transfer to a wire rack to cool.

You will need:

150g butter (soft)
450g icing sugar
3 tablespoons
  cocoa powder
3 tablespoons milk
1 drop red food
  colouring

A large mixing bowl
A small bowl
A food processor

Then make the icing:

1 Cream the butter and icing sugar together in the food processor and put in the mixing bowl.

2 Put two tablespoons of the mixture in a small bowl and mix with a drop of red food colouring until pink. Put to one side.

JOIN IN!

3 Add the milk and cocoa powder to the main mixture and mix well with a rubber spatula.

Turn the page to find out how to decorate your cake!

Now turn your cake into the Gruffalo!
You can copy the picture below.

You will need:

1 black liquorice
    lace
2 big orange sweets
1 small green sweet
5 purple sweets
Black writing icing
150g white marzipan

A sharp knife

What to do:

1 When the cake is completely cold use
  a sharp knife to cut it into the shape
  of the Gruffalo's head. See diagram below.

2 Use the pieces you have cut away to make
  two ears and stick in place with icing.

3 Cover the cake in chocolate icing.

JOIN IN! 4 Gently scrape the back of a fork all over
  the cake to give the icing a rough texture.

JOIN IN! 5 Stick the two orange sweets in place to
  be the Gruffalo's eyes, and stick the small
  green sweet at the end of his nose.

Cut your cake like this:

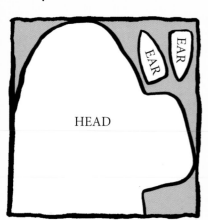

EAR

EAR

HEAD

Copy this picture

6 Cut a liquorice lace into four pieces using a pair of safety scissors. Stick them under the Gruffalo's nose to be his whiskers.

 7 Stick the purple sweets on his back.

8 Pipe black writing icing around the Gruffalo's eyes, and give him pupils and eyebrows. Then pipe a big smile across his face.

9 Use your pink icing to give the Gruffalo's ears a pink middle.

10 Use the marzipan to make two horns, five square teeth and one big curved tusk. Carefully put them in place.

11 Add a glint to his eyes: use marzipan to add a tiny dot to each pupil and a little line on each orange eye.

12 Pipe around the Gruffalo's teeth with black writing icing.

Tips, Tricks and Twists

- You can buy ready-to-use black writing icing in tubes, or make your own and use a piping bag.

- If you put the cooled cake in the freezer for 20 minutes before cutting it into the shape of the Gruffalo's head, you'll find it easier to cut neatly.

- You can use fruit instead of sweets to decorate the Gruffalo: how about purple grapes for prickles, a green grape for a poisonous wart, dried apricots for eyes and banana tusks and teeth?

First published 2016 by Macmillan Children's Books
an imprint of Pan Macmillan
20 New Wharf Road, London N1 9RR
Associated companies throughout the world
www.panmacmillan.com

ISBN: 978-1-5098-0474-0

Recipes copyright © Macmillan Publishers International Limited 2016
Text copyright © Julia Donaldson 1999, 2016
Illustrations copyright © Axel Scheffler 1999, 2010, 2016
Based on the bestselling picture book *The Gruffalo*
by Julia Donaldson and Axel Scheffler
Moral rights asserted.

5 7 9 8 6

A CIP catalogue record for this book is available from the British Library.

Printed in China